# Prayer Shawl
## Ponderings

Prayer Shawl Ponderings

ISBN: 978-1-60920-010-7

Printed in the United States of America

©2010 by Karen Doolaard

Cover design by Isaac Publishing, Inc.

Interior design by Isaac Publishing, Inc.


Library of Congress Cataloging-in-Publication Data


IPI

Isaac Publishing, Inc.

P.O. 342

Three Rivers, MI 49093

www.isaacpublishing.com

Please direct your inquiries to admin@isaacpublishing.com

# Prayer Shawl Ponderings

## Devotions for those who make prayer shawls

by

## Karen Doolaard

Isaac Publishing, Inc.

PO Box 342

Three Rivers, MI 49093

1.888.273.4JOY

www.isaacpublishing.com

# ENDORSEMENTS

"Karen shared a few of her devotionals with me and although the title references prayer shawls these devotionals can pertain to many more aspects of daily life. I believe anyone who has a hobby could relate to what Karen says in her messages. I believe I will re-read these many times because each time I read through this booklet I will find more to "ponder"! I am looking forward to reading more of Karen's thought provoking messages. My prayer for Karen is that God will continue to use her talents to minister to others."

—Sherma Santure

"When Jesus spoke in parables He always compared practical everyday experiences with the heavenly meaning He was explaining – that is what Karen's devotionals do for me as she compares Bible verses with everyday experiences."

—Juella Boerman

"The devotions inspired me and it was time I spent with God. While my hook went in and out, I was praying to have enough yarn and hope the colors are nice for the receivers of the prayer shawl."

—Anne Barnes

"Only God through His Holy Spirit is able to lay on one's heart the kind of thought stimulating illustrations that Karen Doolaard has embraced in her "Prayer Shawl Ponderings."

Comforting, encouraging and challenging, this devotional booklet is relevant to those crafting a prayer shawl as well as anyone willing to ponder God's interweaving in our lives. Thanks, Karen, for following His leading."

—Marge Koeman

"Karen takes the practical work of knitting and crocheting and weaves Biblical perspectives and everyday life applications into the mix of needles, hooks and yarn."

—Jodi Geurink

"Karen's devotionals are very uplifting. It is encouraging to remember that God gives us chances to "do over." I also enjoyed her thoughts on Heaven. I hope many will have the opportunity to enjoy Karen's devotionals."

—Bev Schultz

# ACKNOWLEDGMENTS

Thanks to all of you who have encouraged me in this journey of writing down the devotions that God has instilled in my heart. I am the instrument that He is using to get the words down and I pray for obedience for myself when He sends them-even in the middle of the night!

Many thanks to:
The prayer shawl group at Central Wesleyan church who were my testing ground. I read the devotions at the meetings and got so much positive encouragement to write the words down.

The Thursday morning Bible study group at Ebeneezer Reformed church that gave me new insights into different verses, ideas and concepts.

The ladies in the therapy pool that gave words of encouragement and pushed me on to get the devotionals in book form.

Viv for being a good listener, encourager, prayer warrior and friend.

John, my husband, friend, confidant. I'm sure glad you let me marry you!

Thank you, Lord, for putting all these wonderful people in my life!

# CONTENTS

# VISIBLE AND INVISIBLE

*For by Him all things were created; things in heaven and on earth, visible and invisible, whether thrones or powers or rulers or authorities; all things were created by Him and for Him.* —Colossians 1:16

Recently I heard the phrase, "I'm going to do something visible for the invisible One." Our prayer shawls are definitely something visible that we are doing for God and for others. It certainly is a visible thing by our human standards. We enjoy doing things for other people that are noticed by others and we get some nice compliments on what we are doing.

Have we thought about what invisible things we can do for Him that we are certain we will not get public acclaim for? Those little, quiet things we can do for people that are so helpful to the recipient. These things are not very visible to the human eye but are very visible to God. Lending a helping hand wherever we see a need, bringing a meal, being an emotional support to someone who feels so alone in the world, a quick phone call to say "Hi" or a short visit are all things we can do.

The challenge is to find these invisible things to do, quietly do them and keep them only visible to God.

1

# PONDERINGS

"

"

# PACK RATS

> Do not store up for yourselves treasures on earth, where moth and rust destroy, and where thieves break in and steal. But store up for yourselves treasures in heaven, where moth and rust do not destroy, and where thieves do not break in and steal. For where your treasure is, there your heart will be also. —Matthew 6:19-21

Have you checked your yarn supply lately? You know the bags setting on the floor because there is no room in the yarn cupboard for more! Those bags that had to come in the house while your husband watched TV! We yarn mongrels just cannot pass up a red tag on a skein of yarn because, "It's on sale!" When we are ready to make a shawl, we still need to buy a matching or contrasting color to make it look, "just right!" We aren't aware of how much we have until we have to move to another house or the basement gets flooded and we have to throw out yarn that got wet. We could take the phrase and make it our own, "She who dies with the most yarn, wins!" We aren't sure what she wins but she sure had fun buying the yarn! Ah, so much yarn, so little time!

Proverbs 31 gives us the job description of a wife of noble character and verse 13 tells us *"She selects wool and flax and works with eager hands."* We need to think ahead and buy on sales but not to the point that we need to get a larger cupboard, room or house to hold all our "buys"! Then we need to put those eager hands to work and make that yarn into useful things.

Is our treasure in our yarn? We now have an opportunity to use the talents of knitting, crocheting and buying yarn and use it for a ministry. We shouldn't justify buying yarn by saying it is for a ministry. Is our treasure in the yarn or in the time, talent and prayer it takes to make a shawl? We need to continually set our eyes on Jesus and know that with Him in heaven is where our hearts are.

# PONDERINGS

"

"

## PONDERINGS

"

"

# HANDS TO WORK, HEARTS TO GOD

❝ Make it your ambition to lead a quiet life, to mind your own business and to work with your hands, just as we told you.❞ —I Thessalonians 4:11

The human hand is the most flexible part of the skeleton and has a total of 27 bones in it. That is a lot of bones to keep healthy as well as the muscles and tendons to keep the hand functioning well and without pain. We take it so for granted that our hands will work when we want them to. Two hands are vital to being able to knit and crochet. We crafters will work a long time with sore hands before we give up because of the pain.

In this verse the Thessalonians were taking undue interest in other people's affairs because of idleness. The Greeks in general thought manual labor degrading and fit only for slaves. Christian's took seriously the need for earning their own living, but some of the Thessalonians, perhaps as a result of their belief in the imminent return of Christ, were neglecting work and relying on others to support them. That brings to mind the work ethic of some people today.

It is interesting to study people's hands and consider what

their occupation is or has been. Some are callused and stained from the work they do but can be so gentle when touching someone they love. Hands come in many sizes as well. My paternal grandfather had very large hands. When I looked at my grandmothers hands, I would think of all the bread they kneaded, cloths they washed, babies they held and comforted and diapers they changed. My paternal grandmother raised 12 children and my maternal grandmother raised 10 children. There wasn't much time for idleness in their lives.

Making prayer shawls is a good way to keep our hands busy. It should keep our minds busy and our tongues from idle words. While we keep our hands busy we keep our thoughts on praying for the person we are making the shawl for. Our hands are God's hands in this world. Ecclesiastes 9:10 tells us, *"Whatever your hand finds to do, do it with all your might, for in the grave, where you are going, there is neither working nor planning nor knowledge nor wisdom."* May we remain diligent in our work so we may hear our Lord say, *"Well done, good and faithful servant."*

# PONDERINGS

"

"

# PONDERINGS

"

_____

_____

_____

_____

_____

_____

_____

_____

_____

_____

_____

_____

_____

_____

_____

_____

_____

_____

_____

_____

_____

_____

_____

_____

"

# MY CUP OVERFLOWS

**❝**...You anoint my head with oil, my cup overflows.**❞**

—Psalm 23:5b

My maternal grandmother had Parkinson-like tremors in her hands. When we visited my grandparents, we would all sit around the kitchen table when adults would have coffee. Grandma would pour some of her coffee into her saucer to let it cool. Then, with her trembling hands, she would raise the saucer to her lips and drink her cooled coffee. My brothers, sister and I would watch as she did this and marvel that she did not spill a drop. We would try to drink something from a saucer when we got home and found out how difficult that is to do without spilling.

When I think about Grandma drinking from her saucer, I think about how our cups overflow with blessings into our saucer. The cup is a metaphor for what a host offers his guest when entertaining. God offers a cup of blessing and salvation to a Christian. The wicked drink from a cup of wrath and judgment. Our blessings are numerous! We take our freedom to worship so for granted! We can attend what church we choose, move about freely in the country without accounting to government of our whereabouts. We don't know life to be any different than this. So we hardly think of it as being a blessing because we take it for granted.

It is still amazing that we have loved to crochet and knit for so many years and now we can use that hobby as part of a ministry that reaches out to hurting people. It is a blessing for us that our hands and arms work well so we can crochet and knit. Our eyesight is good to be able to see what we are doing. Psalm 119:171 says, *"May my lips overflow with praise."* Some days we struggle to see our cup as half full instead of half empty. It is so easy to focus on the negative things in life and just take the blessings and positive things for granted. May our prayer be to see our cups not only half full but overflowing into our saucers.

# PONDERINGS

"

"

# PONDERINGS

"

"

# ANGELS UNAWARE

“Do not forget to entertain strangers, for by so
doing some people have entertained angels
without knowing it.” —Hebrews 13:2

Have you ever thought about one of the shawls you make
being one of the swaddling cloths that Mary lovingly
wrapped around Jesus when he was born? Or being part of
Jesus' wardrobe as he ministered here on earth? Or one of
the garments of Jesus that the Roman's cast lots for while
Jesus hung on the cross? What an honor that would be!

We don't know who our shawls are being made for but God
surely does and He knows what a blessing they are. Abraham
(Genesis 18), Gideon (Judges 6) and Minoah (Judges 13)
entertained angels without knowing it. We reach out to
hurting people with our shawls and hurting is not a respector
of persons! It doesn't matter our station in life, we will hurt
at one time or another. Our shawls are just one way that we
can reach out to one another to help along the journey of
life. And in reaching out we may be Jesus to others but they
may be Jesus to us as well. There is a story about a person
who prayed to see Jesus and during the prayer three different
people were brought to his door. The person ministered to

each of them but still prayed to see Jesus. Jesus told the person that He had been at his door three times and was ministered to each time. In Luke 24:13-29, Jesus walks and talks with two men on the road to Emmaus. After the men asked Jesus to stay and share a meal with them, then Jesus revealed Himself to them. Sometimes He seems to leave us because He wants us to ask Him to stay. We don't know, it might be Jesus in the form of each of those people we reach out to with a shawl.

Jesus typically doesn't present Himself as royalty, wealthy or high standing in society. He comes in humility, an "every day" sort of person. May we have the wisdom and vision to see Jesus in those around us!

# PONDERINGS

"

"

# PONDERINGS

"

"

# THREE IN ONE

One of the basic patterns to knit a prayer shawl is to knit 3 stitches and purl 3 stitches. To make crochet granny squares includes 3 double crochet to make a cluster. These patterns are using 3 stitches to create a pattern and can represent faith, hope and love (I Corinthians 12) or the Trinity—God the Father, God the Son and God the Holy Spirit. Each one of the three are needed to make the whole.

A lady in our Bible study taught Sunday School for many years and she used the egg as her example to explain the Trinity. The shell, yolk and white each being a part of the egg and all together making one. My husband uses the example that he is a son, husband and father but he is one person.

The word Trinity is not used in the Bible but they are all three mentioned many times. In Mark 1:10-11 all three persons of the Trinity are involved when Jesus is baptized by John. God the Father speaks, God the Son is baptized and God the Holy Spirit descends on the Son in the form of a dove. Matthew 28:19 gives us the great commission, *"Therefore go and make disciples of all nations, baptizing them in the name of the Father and of the Son and of the Holy Spirit."*

God has always been, even before the world was created. God is supreme over all including thrones or powers or rulers or authorities. How comforting to us in this turbulent time in our world that God is in control of it all! God sent His Son, Jesus, to become one of us and dwell here with us for a time and to suffer a horrible death for us, to save us from our sins. *"He is the image of the invisible God, the firstborn over all creation. For by Him all things were created; things in heaven and on earth, visible and invisible, whether thrones or powers or rulers or authorities; all things were created by Him and for Him."* (Colossians 1:16) After Jesus ascended into heaven, the gift of the Holy Spirit was given to us. The Holy Spirit is an invisible presence here on earth, comforting us and helping us until our work on earth is done.

# PONDERINGS

"

"

# PONDERINGS

"

„

# WORDS

&#x201C; If I speak in the tongues of men and of angels,
but have not love, I am only a resounding gong
or a clanging cymbal.&#x201D;  —I Corinthians 13:1

In the movie "My Fair Lady" the leading lady, Eliza Doolittle,
sings a song about "words, words, words, show me!" She is
tired of Professor Higgins telling her how to say words but
not showing her any feelings. We are so busy saying nice
words but then our actions do not show that we care. As the
saying goes, "Your actions speak so loudly, I can't hear what
you say."

When we show someone a new stitch or pattern to knit or
crochet, we can explain with many words but until we pick
up the yarn and needles/hook and show them, it remains a
mystery. Some people are unable to read patterns so they are
able to look at a stitch or completed shawl and duplicate them.
All the written words in the world are not helpful to them.

Proverbs 10:19 tells us, *"When words are many, sin is not
absent, but he who holds his tongue is wise."* We don't deal
with silence very well. We have to be talking and sometimes
it is about nothing. Then we say things that lead us into

trouble! Abraham Lincoln said, *"It is better to remain silent and be thought a fool, than to speak and remove all doubt."* Then there is Teddy Roosevelt who said, *"Speak softly and carry a big stick"* but I don't think we need to go there!

When delivering shawls to hurting people, we must carefully weigh our words. We want to speak and make them feel loved but there is a time for silence and listening as well. Grieving people can feel more love from your presence with them than from many flowery, well meaning words that are meant to comfort. I struggle with what to say to people who have lost loved ones. Having experienced a loss, I felt most cared for by their presence at the visitation, funeral and cards of sympathy and encouragement.

*"And whatever you do, whether in word or deed, do it all in the name of the Lord Jesus, giving thanks to God the Father through Him"* (Colossians 3:17). Our shawls are our deed that we do in the name of Jesus, may our words be words of love to each other a well as the hurting people we are reaching out to.

# PONDERINGS

"

"

# PONDERINGS

"

"

# DO OVER

> But the pot he was shaping from the clay was marred in his hands; so the potter formed it into another pot, shaping it as seemed best to him.
>
> —Jeremiah 18:4

Many times we start to make something out of yarn and then decide that particular yarn isn't right for that project, wrong size hook or needle, the pattern didn't work with that yarn and many other reason. Sometimes we have made so many mistakes it is easier to take it apart than to try to fix the mistakes. We have the privilege to take it apart and make something else from that yarn. Sometimes I wonder if I will wear out the yarn before it becomes something useful.

God gives us those choices in life. We can have "do overs' in many things in life. The Lord retains the right of limiting His own absolute sovereignty on the basis of human response to His offers of pardon and restoration and His threats of judgment and destruction. But that is on the condition that man's response is to want to change. The yarn or clay doesn't have that choice but we as God's children have the free will to ask God's forgiveness and want to "do over."

God is very patient for us to choose to change. Sometimes He has to allow us to come to the very end of what we can do and then know that only He can do it for us. We repeatedly give it to Him to take care of but then we take it back. Like God needs our help! May our prayer be as the song says,

> *"Have Thine own way, Lord,*
> *Have Thine own way.*
> *Thou art the potter,*
> *I am the clay.*
> *Mold me and make me,*
> *After Thy will*
> *While I am waiting,*
> *Yielded and still."*
> —George C. Stebbins

# PONDERINGS

"

"

# PONDERINGS

"

„

# HEAVEN

❝ So we fix our eyes not on what is seen, but on what is unseen. For what is seen is temporary, but what is unseen is eternal. ❞ —II Corinthians 4:18

Do you think about what heaven will be like? The usual thought is about streets of gold, mansions all prepared which, I assume, means they are furnished with everything we could ever need. There is no marriage or giving in marriage so then no family groups. We will all know each other equally. A man that sang in a quartet with my Dad didn't think he would want to always be singing. My husband is a builder but the mansions are all prepared. He also likes to hunt, will he be getting meat for the table? I am a nurse and I doubt there will be a need for any medical care. Will there be a group of crafty crocheters and noble knitters sitting together making projects? There will be no concern for the cost of yarn or what to do with their finished projects.

My brother passed away at age 52 and his greatest longing was to stay here on earth and farm. Maybe he is farming perfectly in heaven without concern for machinery malfunction, weedless fields and no manure spreaders. People who love to cook will be able to do so without thought of cost of food or if they have the right ingredients for the recipe they want to make. Maybe they won't even need a recipe! Will they have to wash dishes? And there will be lots of us who will be willing to sample their completed items! It doesn't seem like our body appearance will be an issue. Our weight, height, big noses, or big ears will all be a part of who we are—perfectly! And we will never grow old! Will our bodies look like what they did when we die? Minus the aches and pains and physical deformities. Will babies be babies in heaven? Just think of all the generations of people we will be with and know all their names!

We look at heaven with earthy limited eyesight and understanding. This earth, as we know it, is a temporary, fleeting thing. Half the fun of an event or vacation is the planning and anticipation of doing it. Why not anticipate heaven, where we will spend eternity? To fix our eyes on these visible things would cause us to lose heart. We need to look away from this temporary world and set our sight on heaven. All these terribly important questions we think we have here on earth are not going to matter once we get to heaven. By comparison, the eternal glory is far greater than all the suffering we may face in this life.

# PONDERINGS

"

"

# PONDERINGS

"

"

# SERVANT'S HEART

❝After that, He poured water into a basin and
began to wash His disciples' feet, drying them
with the towel that was wrapped around Him.❞

—John 13:5

As knitters and crocheters we are very content to sit quietly
doing our project and not be looking for front, center stage
attention. We enjoy our quiet project and ponderings.
We are praying about who to give this shawl to as well as
for them, if we know who the shawl is going to be given to.
All this is very good IF we have the right attitude in our
heart.

Jesus is doing a very menial task of washing His disciples
feet to show us how we should be willing to be humble
enough to do a servant's job. In John 1:27 it talks about being
willing to fasten thongs on someone else's sandals. That was
considered a servant's job as well. No job or activity is more
or less important in the Kingdom but what is most important
is the attitude of our hearts. Are we doing it for the glory
we will receive from fellow human beings? Or are we doing
it to honor God and care for *"the least of these"* (Matthew
25:49)? It is wonderful to receive these "warm fuzzies" from

other people and we need to encourage each other. But that must not be our motive to do something for someone else.

Along the path of life, God may ask us to do hard and difficult things. We may fight it, work around it and try to avoid it. Finally, when we submit to His will for what He is asking of us, He does not always require us to do the hard thing, He just wants us to be willing to do it for Him. He wants our hearts to be in the right attitude so He can work through us.

# PONDERINGS

"

"

# PONDERINGS

"

"

# TRANSFORMED

> " Do not conform any longer to the pattern of this world, but be transformed by the renewing of your mind. Then you will be able to test and approve what God's will is – His good, pleasing and perfect will. "
> —Romans 12:2

When we start working on a shawl, we start with a new skein of yarn. The first challenge is getting the end from the center that pulls out and unravels the skein from the inside out. Sometimes it comes out in a knotted mass and we need to take the time to untangle that before we can even start working on the shawl. Then we begin knitting or crocheting and the skein of yarn becomes transformed into a thing of usefulness and beauty.

Every inch of yarn in that skein will go through our fingers as it is being transformed, one stitch at a time, into the pattern we have chosen. Occasionally we have tangles in the yarn and we have to lay aside our project to untangle the yarn. That appears to be non-productive to finishing our projects but it is all part of the process. Those knots in life appear non-productive but that is when we are the most teachable and we learn to lean harder into our Lord. It puts us in God's waiting room for a time or leads us to work on other areas of life that need attention. Transforming is a process not a single event.

It is satisfying to come to the end of a skein of yarn but that is when it is more likely to tangle as the outer layers of yarn collapse on themselves. We are anxious to complete that skein but we again have to lay aside our work and untangle. But completing one skein does not complete the shawl! We move on to the next skein, search for that elusive end to the start of the skein and work our way through that skein, one stitch at a time.

Our lives are a continuous spiritual transformation that lead to what God wants from each of us as believers. His perfect will! This leads to our spiritual and moral growth and that is pleasing to God, not necessarily to us. This may include "knots" for us to untangle and slow us up in reaching our goal but makes us more fit to become perfect, to fit the will of God and His goal for us.

# PONDERINGS

"

"

# PONDERINGS

"

"

# A QUICK PRAYER

In the business of life, I was rushing through my day. As I sat down in the evening, I picked up the prayer shawl I was working on while I watched TV. Then I remembered I needed to pray while I do this. "God, bless whoever is going to get this shawl!" Then I began to think about what I had just prayed.

God – I am asking the Almighty God to be with me as I make each stitch. His presence is with me now and always but I asked for an audience with Him right now. I feel His hands on mine as I make each stitch and He is working in my heart as I think about who might receive this shawl.

Bless – I am asking for God's richest blessing on this person. If it is health, emotional needs, loneliness, dealing with the death of a loved one or someone with a terminal illness. I don't know those things, but God does. I am blessed to be able to make this shawl and pray that the receiver may be blessed as well.

Whoever – In this big world of millions of people I am praying for one person who will receive this shawl. God knows them personally. I may know them briefly or a long time friend.

Is — That person is a part of this world right now. We are such a fleeting breath in this world but God chose for me to be a part of this world when this person is also a part of this world. I pray that I may bless their little corner of this world.

Going — I am assuming I will be here tomorrow to give this shawl to someone. We don't know what our future is or anyone else. We are busy going but we are choosing to take time to make a shawl for someone and to spend time with them when we give them the shawl.

Get — All this "stuff" that we think we need in this world! But we are making something that is earthly but has heavenly meaning. Weave many prayers into this earthly shawl!

This — I am praying for THIS shawl and THIS person. I am focusing on just THIS one right now! I need tunnel vision right now. God sees us each as an individual and not one of many.

Shawl — It really is just a lot of stitches all put together. But I am asking God that whoever receives this shawl will feel Jesus' arms around them when they put this shawl on. May they feel His warmth, His touch and the peace of God in their hearts.

Even our short, quick prayers can have a lot of meaning!

# PONDERINGS

"

"

# PONDERINGS

"

"

# PRAYER SHAWL

"The Lord said to Moses, "Speak to the Israelites and say to them; Throughout the generations to come you are to make tassels on the corners of your garment, with a blue cord on each tassel. You will have these tassels to look at and so you will remember all the commands of the Lord, that you may obey them and not prostitute yourselves by going after the lusts of your own hearts and eyes. Then you will remember to obey all my commands and will be consecrated to your God."
—Numbers 15:37-40

The original Old Testament prayer shawl had a lot of symbolism attached to it. The tassels were to be attached at the four corners to remind them of God's law. As one would walk along, the tassels would swirl about at the edge of his garment, serving as excellent memory prods to obey God's commands. There are other reminders coded into the fringes. The 613 commandments of the Torah as well as other messages contained within the tying of the fringes. Before putting on the shawl the benediction is recited: *"Blessed are Thou, O Lord our God, King of the universe, who hast hallowed us by Thy commandments, and hast commanded us to enwrap ourselves in the fringed garment."* There are other benedictions that different sects use.

Matthew 6:6 tells us to enter into our "closet" for prayer. When a Jewish man puts on his prayer shawl, he closes himself in and shuts out the world. This effectively becomes his "prayer closet."

In Numbers 15:38 it tells us there is to be a ribband of blue. The blue dye was very difficult to obtain and therefore expensive. The shawl is usually white and made of wool or silk and ideally be long enough to cover most of the body.

We have taken a lot of liberties with our prayer shawls of today. We try to avoid tassels because the yarn we use frays and tangles up in the tassels. The tassels are also a problem with people who are in wheelchairs as they get caught in the wheels. We have patterns for them to be triangular as well as rectangular. We use a lot of different colors and do not make a point of putting a blue stripe through each one. We want the receiver to feel the prayers that were said in their behalf while the shawl was being made, to feel the arms of Jesus around them and to nestle in the warmth of the shawl as well as the love of fellow believers and, most of all, God's love.

# PONDERINGS

"

"

# PONDERINGS

"

"

# GOD'S DELIGHT

" The Lord your God is with you,
He is mighty to save.
He will take great delight in you,
He will quiet you with His love,
He will rejoice over you with singing. "

—Zephaniah 3:17

As you sit there knitting or crocheting your prayer shawl, God is with you! He knows your heart as you work and pray on your shawl. As you take the yarn and wrap it around your hook or needle, so God is wrapping His arms around you and the person you are making it for. You are molding the yarn just as God is molding you to do great things for Him.

God takes great delight in each of us. The dictionary's explanation of delight is "to affect with great pleasure, to please highly, to give or afford high satisfaction or joy. Take great pleasure, to be greatly pleased or rejoiced." Think of all those adjectives describing how God feels about us! Try to think about something that you take great pleasure and delight in. And that is how excited God is about each one of us!

Then He will quiet us with His love! Crocheting and knitting are quiet activities. That gives us lots of time to think about God, who we are making the shawl for, activities of the day, etc. I find it very beneficial to put spiritual music on while I work on my shawl. It leads me down different paths of thought about God and His world. God can quiet me with the music as well as rejoice over me with singing! What music we listen to and what things we read is what fills our minds throughout the day. When we fill our minds with thoughts of God, we can have His peace in our hearts.

Know that God is taking great delight in you!

# PONDERINGS

"

"

# PONDERINGS

"

"

# THE WEAVER

" My life is but a weaving
  Between my Lord and me,
  I cannot choose the colors
  He worketh steadily.

  Oftimes He weaveth sorrow,
  And I in foolish pride
  Forget He sees the upper
  And I, the underside.

  Not till the loom is silent
  And the shuttles cease to fly
  Shall God unroll the canvas
  And explain the reason why.

  The dark threads are as needful
  In the Weaver's skillful hand
  As the threads of gold and silver
  In the pattern He has planned. "

—Grand Colfax Tuller

God allows us so many choices in life! What occupation,
where we live, who we marry, how many children we have

and so much more. But He is ultimately in control of what happens in our lives.

We can choose the color of yarn we choose to make our shawls with. When we choose a variegated yarn we can compare the light and the dark to the different things that happen in our lives. The variegated yarn makes it's own design— sometimes stripes, sometimes a wavy solid design down the middle of the shawl or just colors every which way with no apparent design. So is life! It makes it's own design! The dark colors may be compared to dark, sad times in our lives, the light to the happier, more pleasant times. They appear to us to be just happening but God is in control of it all.

Most of these things we won't find answers to in this life. And when we get to heaven with our list of questions, it isn't going to matter anymore! We will enjoy the silver and gold of our pattern then!

But all these colors and patterns are needful in shawls as well as life. One hooks onto the other and crates the whole picture. We wouldn't enjoy the rainbow without the rain, we enjoy happier times more after we experience sad, darker times. We are being refined by God through life.

# PONDERINGS

"

"

# PONDERINGS

"

"

# MORNING MIST

**"** You are a mist that appears for a little while and then vanishes. **"**                    —James 4:14b

Our lives are compared to a mist in this passage. It reminds us again how quickly passing our lives are. It is figuratively referring to that which is temporary. Hosea 6:4b says, *"Your love is like the morning mist, like the early dew that disappears."* We focus on how temporary our lives here on earth are. By earthly standards, 80 to 90 years is a long time but in light of eternity it is a brief mist.

Mist is a very beneficial and nurturing thing. It gives moisture and nourishment to the ground and growing things. In a dry climate, that is life saving. The visible mist is fleeting but its effects are long lasting.

Are our lives just the brief mist that is here and gone so quickly or are we nourishing, feeding and caring for those around us? What is our legacy? Is it material things that we wish to pass along to the next generation or are we looking to pass along wisdom and knowledge of God and His word?

Giving a prayer shawl to a person is a tangible thing to give them that reminds them of others who are praying for them. This can be great encouragement to someone who is to physically weak or discouraged to be able to pray for themselves. It also represents the caring and nourishing that we as Christians can do for each other as well as reaching out to those who have not made Jesus the Lord of their life.

# PONDERINGS

"

"

# PONDERINGS

"

"

# FIRST FRUITS

"We give Thee but Thine own, What're the gift
may be,
All that we have is Thine alone, A trust, O Lord,
from Thee.

My we Thy bounties thus as stewards true receive,
And gladly, as Thou blessest us, To Thee our
first-fruits give.

To comfort and to bless, To find a balm for woe,
To tend the lone and fatherless is angel's work
below."

As we look around an see all the things we are blessed with, we have to acknowledge that it is all from the hand of God. It is on loan to us from God. Nature speaks to us of God's greatness. God allows us so many material things and it is so easy for us to say, "I earned it, I deserve it." But it is only by the grace of God that we have life, the world we live in and all the material things.

In return God asks of us our first-fruits. It may be in material things, our finances, ourselves or our loved ones. My Dad taught us that a collection is the gathering up of left overs and an offering is the giving of our first-fruits. Sometimes He asks of us to give up some of those things. In the economy of today it would seem God is asking us, *"Do you love Me more than these things?"* Sometimes He takes children to Himself before we are ready to let them go. My 80 year old parents struggle with the loss of their 52 year old son. By earthly standards, children shouldn't precede their parents in death.

Our talent of crocheting and knitting is also a gift from God. Now we have an opportunity to use that talent in making prayer shawls that will comfort and bless those we give them to. That puts a higher calling on our talent that we have used for a hobby. Isn't it exciting to use something we love to do and now it can be used to bless and comfort those around us?

# PONDERINGS

"

"

# PONDERINGS

"

"

# GENEROUSLY GIVE,
# GRACIOUSLY RECEIVE

*❝ For God so loved the world that He gave His only begotten Son, that whoever believes in Him shall not perish but have everlasting life. ❞* —John 3:16

Bringing a shawl to a hurting person is so gratifying! We are bringing a tangible item but we are also telling them that we prayed for them while we made the shawl and those prayers are so meaningful to hurting people. It makes us feel very generous and, hopefully, spurs us on to do more things for God and others. We are not saved by good works but for good works.

Receiving a shawl is also a blessing. So frequently we are uncomfortable to be on the receiving end. When we are given a compliment how many of us can just say a grateful "Thank You" and stop at that. We usually feel we need to explain away what we have been complimented on. Frequently the receiver of a shawl will say, "You didn't need to do this." How often do we receive gifts and feel they aren't quite what we wanted and hope to exchange the item? Have we considered what feelings that gives to the giver? What is more important, the actual item we received or the feelings of the giver?

To be a generous giver we need to learn to be a gracious receiver. God GAVE His Son, knowing exactly what was going to happen to Him in His life and His death. So now we HAVE the eternal life that God had planned for us but not without price on Jesus' part. Are we gracious receivers of that eternal life?

# PONDERINGS

"

"

# PONDERINGS

"

"

# YOU'RE THE ONLY JESUS SOME WILL EVER SEE

“ In the same way, let your light shine before men, that they may see your good deeds and praise your Father in heaven. ” —Matthew 5:16

Neither of my grandmother's would knit or crochet on Sunday. Their knitting was usually making socks, hats, scarves and sweaters for their children so it was work for them and that is not how they could honor their Lord on the Lord's day. They wanted to be examples to their children about honoring the Lord's day. Each one of us has a different idea about honoring the Lord on the Lord's day. What is right or wrong for one person is not always correct for another person. And who are we to judge what is right or wrong for another person?

The most important thing in our lives is living our lives to be a witness for God. We are the only Jesus some will ever see. Others should be able to see us and how we respond to life and know that Someone greater is living in us.

When we go on vacation or travel to another area of the country where people don't know us, do we act differently than when we are around people we know? Our lives should be a witness all day every day to be a light in this dark world.

Frequently I have heard about Bible study groups or groups of people who go to a restaurant after church to eat. The waitresses will talk about how rude the people were, how poor they tipped and how inconsiderate they were. Sometimes our actions speak so loud people can't hear what we say. We need to show Jesus to those who are serving us because that may be the only Jesus they will ever see. They have no desire to seek Christianity because what they have seen of Christians isn't very impressive. We are all dressed up in our Sunday finery but what are our actions and words telling others? Does your driving reflect Christ? You may have a bumper sticker that proclaims you are a Christian but you drive like the world owes it to you. Once again, your actions are speaking so loudly I can't hear what you say!

We need to proudly light our lamps for Jesus and set them on a stand for all to see.

# PONDERINGS

"

"

# PONDERINGS

"

"

# PATIENCE

❝So that you may have great endurance and patience.❞  —Colossians 1:11b

That word, patience, is slipped into so many places in the Bible and we so easily read right over it. It is one of the gifts of the Spirit and we are sure that we are practicing it. How do we react when traffic is difficult and we arrive at our destination angry because of it? When we are standing in line at the check out in the store and things aren't moving along like we think they should, how are we handling that? Are we allowing the situation to steal our joy? Are we blooming where we are planted? While standing in line, strike up a conversation with those in line with you. The time sure goes a lot faster, more pleasantly and best of all, we may be Jesus is someone's life right there in the line.

Recently I started a prayer shawl from a pattern that I had made several times. I could not get the edges to come out even. After I had taken it loose for the upteenth time, I persevered and got it right! I wanted to throw it away at times or use a different pattern but when it came out right it felt so good that I had accomplished it.

Our Christian walk seems like a very hard struggle at times. God did not promise life to be easy. Our world today seems to be spinning out of control but we need to step back and know that God is in control. He is allowing all of this to happen. We must not allow the situation to steal our joy. We are running His race and we can use this time to stretch and grow in Him. Revelation 3:10 gives us the promise, *"Since you have kept my command to endure patiently, I will also keep you from the hour of trial that is going to come upon the whole world to test those who live on the earth."*

# PONDERINGS

"

"

# PONDERINGS

"

"

# JOY COMES
# IN THE MORNING

  **Those who sow in tears will reap with songs of joy. He who goes out weeping, carrying seed to sow, will return with songs of joy, carrying sheaves with him.** —Psalm 126:5-6

An elderly lady taught me how to make granny squares and how to crochet them together. We spent an evening together picking out the yarn and then got started on the squares. I went home and made several squares and when I went back for my next lesson, she showed me my mistake of not seeing what was the front and back of the square. I had to take apart several rounds on several squares. That was a hard lesson to learn! But in order to do it correctly, we need to learn to tear it apart as well. Now I am very aware of what the front and back of a crochet stitch look like. Some tears were shed on my part but I sure felt good when I could look at my completed project and know that the stitches were all facing the correct way.

Life hands us those unpleasant things to experience! Death of friends and family , illnesses, hurtful words and deeds are all a part of life. It is our choice if we want to allow them to make us bitter or better. We can choose if we want to dwell on this experience, think negative thoughts or make it a positive learning experience. The toilet needs to be cleaned and we can choose if we want to do it joyfully or grumble because we have such an unpleasant chore to do.

As we are working on our shawl, we are praying and sometimes weeping for the person and the situation that person finds themselves in. God is in that as well. It draws us closer to Him, makes us reach out to others to bring them closer to ourselves and ultimately to God. When things seem to be unraveling just remember Who is knitting all things together for good! We may start our shawl with weeping but our sheaves—shawls—are completed with joy!

# PONDERINGS

"

"

# PONDERINGS

"

"

# JUST THE RIGHT ONE

“ We have different gifts, according to the grace
given us. . .If it is encouraging, let him encourage,
if it is contributing to the needs of others, let him
give generously, if it is leadership, let him govern
diligently; if it is showing mercy, let him do it
cheerfully. ” —Romans 12:6a & 8

Crochet hooks and knitting needles come in many sizes. A
set of crochet hooks can contain 24 hooks starting at double
zero, that is very small, and going up to K, which is the
"jumbo" size. Knitting needles also come in many sizes and
can be circular, double point or single point needles. They
can be made of aluminum, bamboo, plastic, wood or stainless
steel. There are even light up knitting needles and crochet
hooks for the dedicated crafter to work in the dark! Hooks
and needles also come in many different colors.

When we start a new project we frequently will start with a
certain size needle or hook and then find it doesn't make
the look we want, give the tension we want or give the right
gauge. So we tear out what we have made and choose another
size hook or needle and start again. We crafters can be quite
diligent with getting the right look and are willing to take

our project apart a few times to get the right look. We do have our favorite sizes that seem to fit our hands well and make the look we want.

Human beings have been created in many sizes, shapes, colors and have many different talents. God can use each of us just as we are. There is no right or wrong in being an encourager, giving to others, showing mercy to others or serving others. He just wants willing hearts and hands. *"The only thing that counts is faith expressing itself through love"* (Galations 5:6b).

God is choosing the right size hook or needle for His projects as well. We are those tools and He chooses carefully which tool He wants for what project. It is not a one size fits all. God has a special plan (pattern) for each of us. We can be encouragers who reach out to others with an uplifting, cheerful word. We can be contributors by giving of our own or distributing what has been given by others. We can show mercy by caring for the sick, the poor and the aged. Serving the needy should be a delight, not a chore. We may excel in one or more of these things but each gift is important and that we are willing to be the tools for God.

# PONDERINGS

"

„

# PONDERINGS

"

"

# WEAVING ME

“ When I was woven together in the depths of the earth, your eyes saw my unformed body. ”

——Psalm 139:15b

When we start thinking of making a shawl, we check out the patterns and see which one we are wanting to make. Then we check out what yarn we have on hand to see if we have enough and the right color we have in our mind. We are visualizing how it would look and if we know who we are making it for, how they would like it or look with it on. If we don't have the "right" yarn, we go to the store and get what we are visualizing. Through this whole process we are praying for the project, the person who receives it and for us to be a blessing in our work.

Psalm 139 is talking about God and His project of creating us. Not just the whole general population, me, personally! He visualized me physically, emotionally and knew just how He was weaving me together. He knew the color of my skin, color of my hair, color of my eyes, height, weight and how big my feet would be, long before He wove me together. He knew my emotional make up, my sensitive spots, my personality, my wants and desires. Verse 14 says, *"I praise you because I am fearfully and wonderfully made, Your works are wonderful, I know that full well."* He chose my parents and siblings therefor choosing what family I would be born into. He chose what city, state and country I would be born into. And He knew the length of my days here on earth even before He started weaving me. He saved His crowning project until day 6 of creation. Then He rested!

And we think we have a big project going when we are choosing patterns, yarn and who to give our shawl to!

Now it is our responsibility to take care of these bodies and emotions that God so perfectly wove together. Verse 23 and 24 say, *"Search me, O God and know my heart, test me and know my anxious thought, See if there is any offensive way in me and lead me in the way everlasting."* I am asking God to examine me in order to check on the integrity of my devotion and keep me true. It is no light matter to be examined by God. We are our own most critical and loving critique of the shawl we have made. So much more is God in critiquing and loving me as His child.

# PONDERINGS

"

"

# PONDERINGS

"

"

# ENCOURAGING WORDS

" Therefore encourage one another and build each other up, just as in fact you are doing. "

—Hebrews 5:11

The prayer shawl group in our church meets together once a month. It is a delightful time of helping each other with a difficult pattern, comparing yarns, getting a pattern worked out and bringing completed shawls. There is lots of talk about where yarn is on sale and what kinds of yarn different people prefer to use. I enjoy sitting back and just listening to the conversations that are going on and how we all learn from each other. There are so many words of encouragement about what nice work others do, choice of colors and patterns. We have all age groups involved in one common subject. The young come with their new ideas and the older ones come with their experience. This gathering together time is so enriching and when we leave we are excited about what we are doing. We are charged up and ready to go.

God certainly knew what He was doing when He encouraged believers to gather together and encourage each other. In Hebrews 11:25 we are told, *"Let us not give up meeting together, as some are in the habit of doing, but let us encourage one another."* Meeting together is one way to be able to encourage each other. We are such a social world with all our forms of communication. Are we remembering to encourage each other in all those forms of communication?

Isn't it amazing what a word of encouragement can do for each of us? How quickly we can be torn down with discouraging words. How easy it is to give discouraging words instead of encouraging words. We have to make a conscious effort to be encouraging. Many of us were raised in homes where we heard more discouraging words. It is not an easy thing to change that mind set. Colossians 2:6 says, *"So then, just as you received Christ Jesus as Lord, continue to live in Him, rooted and built up in Him, strengthened in the faith as you were taught, and overflowing with thankfulness."* May our encouraging words build others and ourselves up so we overflow with thankfulness to our Lord and Savior!

# PONDERINGS

"

"

# PONDERINGS

"

"

# NESTING

“Jesus replied, 'Foxes have holes and birds of the air have nests, but the Son of Man has no place to lay His head.'” —Matthew 8:20

When someone walks into your living room or family room, can they tell which chair you spend your time in? You know, the one with pattern books, scissors, needles, hooks and a couple prayer shawls in progress laying around it! We crafters like to have our nest that is surrounded with our projects. One gal in our prayer shawl group has about three chairs she sits in and each one has a different prayer shawl in progress beside it. So what chair she sits in determines which shawl she will work on. If there is one shawl she doesn't particularly enjoy working on, she doesn't sit in that chair very often. Most of us just have one chair with several projects in progress.

It is interesting in nature that animals and birds have nests when they have their young but the rest of their lives they are nomads. They will return to the same area to make a nest or den to have their young but they don't call it home or spend time there after their young are old enough to get out. From a human perspective that seems like a "loose" way to live because our identity is so much in where our home is. It gives us a sense of belonging.

We humans are different than the animals in that we have our homes and then we even have a certain chair we migrate to at the end of the day. We take great pride in our homes and that leads to a lot of materialism and competition with other human beings. Matthew 6:26 tells us to *"Look at the birds of the air; they do not sow or reap or store away in barns, and yet your heavenly Father feeds them. Are you not much more valuable than they?"* Our identity should not be in our home or nest but in the One that created us. This sinful old world is not our home, we are passing through to a far better place.

# PONDERINGS

"

"

# PONDERINGS

"

"

# JUST ENOUGH

❝ When all the jars were full, she said to her son, "Bring me another one." But he replied, "There is not a jar left." Then the oil stopped flowing. ❞

—II Kings 4:6 (NIV)

When you choose to make a shawl that changes colors frequently and you are using up different colors, there is a concern that you will have enough of that color to finish a row or a round in the pattern you are making. We find ourselves "praying" that the yarn will last until the row or round is complete. Sometimes we run out of yarn before the end, sometimes we have left over yarn and sometimes it even comes out just right!

So many times in life we would like things to come out just right. But that isn't how life usually is. We run out of money before we run out of time or the other way around. The gauge on the gas tank shows empty before we have the money or time to refill it. We run out of an ingredient before we have enough for a recipe. Or we have to much of one thing or another. To much sunshine, to much rain, to much wind, to much time on our hands.

God makes perfect plans and always allows just enough. If we have to much, we get greedy and want more. If we don't have enough, we whine and cry about that. But God in his infinite wisdom knows what is just enough. How much we can handle emotionally, physically, or spiritually are all part of His perfect plan. From our human perspective it may appear that we are experiencing more than we can endure. God knows what is just enough for each of us. I wish you just enough!

# PONDERINGS

"

"

# PONDERINGS

"

"

# LOOSE ENDS

> It (grace) teaches us to say "No" to ungodliness and worldly passions, and to live self-controlled and godly lives in this present age, while we wait for the blessed hope – the glorious appearing of our great God and Savior, Jesus Christ, who gave Himself for us to redeem us from all wickedness and to purify for Himself a people that are His very own, eager to do what is good.
>
> —Titus 2:12-14

When making a shawl that changes color of yarn frequently there are many ends of yarn that need to be worked in. When making granny squares, I was taught to lay the ends in as I worked the next round. Then when the project is complete, all the ends are worked in as well. A shawl can be made from a beautiful pattern and wonderful workmanship but if the ends are still hanging out it quickly looses it's beauty.

Life has a lot of loose ends and we have to keep working to get them worked in. Unfinished projects are not fun to come back to. It gives a great sense of accomplishment to not only start a project but complete it and see it in it's entirety. Stick-to-itivness is not a trait easily learned. In Titus 2, Paul tells each age group what would be "loose ends" for them to be working on. These are not easy things to work on. Older men need to endure, don't retire from being a Christian. Older women need to teach the next generation. Younger women are to make family a priority. Younger men need to be self controlled. Slaves (employees) are to be honest and trustworthy.

In this text, Paul is telling Titus emphatically that he needs to contrast his work with that of the false teachers. This sound doctrine demands right conduct of all believers, regardless of age, sex or position. Christian living should help rather than hinder the spread of the gospel. We need to work on the "loose ends" that Paul is pointing out to different age groups earlier in this chapter. We as Christians represent our Lord to this world. How we work, behave, and talk is what non-Christians see as representing Christ and Christianity. *"So that in every way they will make the teaching about God our Savior attractive"* (Titus 2:10b). Pick up your hook/needles, tuck in your loose ends and show the world you are a Christian!

# PONDERINGS

"

"

# PONDERINGS

"

"

# PRAYING CONTINUALLY

❝Be joyful always; pray continually; give thanks in all circumstances, for this is God's will for you in Christ Jesus.❞ ——I Thessalonians 5:16-18

For many years I have had the privilege of doing custom crocheting for many people. I have always found this a wonderful time to be in prayer for the person I am making the item for. This was long before prayer shawls were known. I am sure I am not the only person who prays for who they are making an item for. This is true of those who bake special goodies for someone, make a meal for someone, clean someone else's house and many more opportunities we can pray for others. We don't need to "assume the position" of prayer, we just pray as the day goes on and God puts someone in our mind and heart.

Many times I hear others and myself say, "Is all we can do is pray." That is ALL? That should be the first thing we do and that is the greatest thing we can do for a situation. From pillow talk prayers to diligent prayers, all are heard by our Heavenly Father. We may feel frustrated that we need to "do" something physical for a situation but prayer is the biggest "do" we can possibly do.

II Thessalonians 1:11 says, "*With this in mind, we constantly pray for you, that our God may count you worthy of His calling, and that by His power He may fulfill every good purpose of yours and every act prompted by your faith.*" Our act is making a prayer shawl for someone God has laid on our heart. Then give God the glory for giving us the thought to make the shawl, the ability to make the shawl and being able to give that shawl to the person.

We don't always know what to pray for. In Romans 8:26 it tells us, "*In the same way, the Spirit helps us in our weakness. We do not know what we ought to pray for, but the Spirit Himself intercedes for us with groans that words cannot express.*" We don't always know who we are making the shawl for so we don't know who or what to pray for. God sorts that out for us, better than we could if we knew.

# PONDERINGS

"

"

# PONDERINGS

"

"

# BODY OF BELIEVERS

"Just as each of us has one body with many members, and these members do not all have the same function, so in Christ we who are many form one body, and each member belongs to all the others." —Romans 12:4-5

Recently my friend, Lynette, sent three skeins of yarn that were different shades of blue. I chose to make a prayer shawl out of the yarn and chose a pattern called, "Hugs and Kisses" that another friend, Ann, had given me. Ann is one of the ladies that are in the therapy pool at the local aquatic center where I go. I made the shawl and ran out of one of the shades of blue. I talked to Ann about it because I had recently had surgery and could not get to a store to find matching yarn. Ann took a sample of the yarn and got a skein that matched. I completed the shawl and put it in the closet.

About a week later another friend from the pool, Dorothy, called and said she wanted to send a prayer shawl to Penny, a gal that had been in the pool for a time while she was home on leave from her job as a missionary in Ireland. So Dorothy came to our house and of all the shawls she chose the blue one to send to Penny. Penny has had many different health problems and was now having treatment for more health issues. Dorothy sent the shawl to Penny in Ireland.

Each of these ladies come from different backgrounds. Lynette has been my friend since grade school and we have kept up the relationship and it grows closer and stronger as the years go by. Lynette attends the Evangelical Free Church. Ann grew up in Germany during World War II and immigrated to the United States as an adult. Ann attends the Methodist Church. Dorothy grew up in England and met her American husband when he was stationed there during World War II. They married and moved to the United States. She attends the Episcopal Church. I grew up in South Dakota and moved to Michigan when I got married. I attend the Wesleyan Church.

Four women were involved in this prayer shawl—buying yarn, getting the pattern, making and giving it to someone. We each have different abilities and saw different needs that we could do something about. Look at the different backgrounds but they all had one thing in common. Reaching out to someone who is hurting in the name of Christ.

# PONDERINGS

"

"

## PONDERINGS

"

"

# GOOD FOUNDATION

My paternal grandmother would buy her yarn wrapped in a
large loop and it would need to be rolled into balls. My brother
and I would be at Grandma's house for piano lessons and
when they were finished she would get out the yarn. One of
us would hold our arms out and then the loop of yarn would
be slipped on the hands and the other would start wrapping
it into a ball. The yarn on the ball must not be wrapped to
tight as that would stretch the yarn. It needed to be wrapped
neatly so the ball wouldn't fall apart. My brother and I would
get the giggles at times and not pay attention to what we were
doing and Grandma would correct us and get us back on task.
How we took care of the yarn made a difference in how the
project that Grandma used it for would turn out.

The beginning row of knitting or crocheting also determines
how tight, loose, long, short and the correct number of
stitches our project will be. We are laying the foundation for
our project.

There are many references in the Bible about laying the cornerstone and foundation of material things. This then leads to the cornerstone and foundation of our faith. A firm foundation stands the test of time. We are to use good workmanship in anything we set our hands to doing. Colossians 3:23 tells us, *"Whatever you do, work at it with all your heart, as working for the Lord, not for men."* We need the mind of Christ in everything we do.

# PONDERINGS

"

"

# PONDERINGS

"

"

# WRAPPED IN HIS SHAWL

> " Since you have kept my command to endure
> patiently, I will also keep you from the hour of
> trial that is going to come upon the whole world
> to test those who live on the earth. "
>
> —Revelation 3:10

In this text it feels like God is wrapping His shawl around us as believers. In this crazy, mixed up world that we live in it is reassuring to be reminded that God is in control. Our world feels like it is spinning out of control. We are commanded to endure patiently, stand firm in our faith and He will keep us through. The hour of trial is the period of testing that precedes the consummation of the kingdom. Matthew 24:12-13 says, *"Because of the increase of wickedness, the love of most will grow cold, but he who stands firm to the end will be saved."*

What a wonderful place to be wrapped in Jesus' shawl and held safely by Him. It doesn't remove us from this world, it just holds us in the world. We are to be in the world but not of the world. Our human nature would have us escape from the world to Jesus but we have work to do here. Matthew 24:14 tells us *"And this gospel of the kingdom will be preached in the whole world as a testimony to all nations, and then the end will come."* We need to get the gospel to all the world before Jesus will come. They may not accept the gospel but we are required that they at least know about the gospel before Jesus will return.

We put on the armor of God and press onward in the battle of life and spreading the gospel. God gives us the reassurance of the warmth of the shawl that He is with us in this battle.

# PONDERINGS

"

"

# PONDERINGS

"

"

# LONG TERM MEMORY

❝ Remember the former things, those of long ago;
I am God, and there is no other; I am God, and
there is none like Me. ❞ —Isaiah 46:9

We enjoy playing Mexican train dominos with friends. We talk about learning to play the game well now so we can remember how to play the game when we are older and struggle with memory loss. My Dad is living with Alzheimer's and has a hard time remembering things. But when someone asks him to pray in a group setting, he can pray so sincerely and there is no memory loss then. He has been a praying man all his life and we thank God for that example in our lives.

Growing up with four siblings, we each took our turn praying out loud after the meal. We all learned to pray out loud and that was a good learning experience. Praying out loud is difficult for some people. If we learn to do it as children, it is easier to do as an adult and as we grow older it is part of our long term memory.

All the knitting and crocheting we do should sure be sinking into our long term memory! It is interesting how often I have to look up the pattern for a project that I have made several times and have to refresh my memory of the pattern. Then I am amazed to find what patterns come naturally if I relax and let it come.

How comforting to have a God that is the same yesterday, today and forever! We don't have to depend on long term memory because He is daily moving in our lives and our world. May He be the center of our long term and short term memory!

# PONDERINGS

"

"

# PONDERINGS

"

"

# AMEN

**❝...to the only wise God be glory forever through Jesus Christ! Amen.❞** —Romans 16:27

The dictionary defines amen as *"a term occurring generally at the end of a prayer and meaning 'so be it'."* Our prayers usually end with amen but are we thinking what it means. The seven fold amen from Handel's Messiah is a magnificent thing to listen to as well as to sing. A beautiful 4 part harmony Amen at the end of a hymn is so worshipful. Revelation 5:14 says, *"The four living creatures said, 'Amen' and the elders fell down and worshipped."* That is where Handel got his inspiration for the seven fold amen. *"To Him who sits on the throne and to the Lamb be praise and honor and glory and power for ever and ever!"* (Revelation 5:13b). Just reading that verse makes me want to say amen!

The quietly whispered, "Amen" while someone is praying or during a message at church gives validation to the one who is speaking as well as affirmation of what is being said. A quietly raised hand can also say a silent amen. When the ride home has been very nerve racking with weather or busy traffic, once safely at home it is easy to whisper, "Thank You, Lord, Amen!"

As I was researching to write this devotional, I found it interesting that the word amen is not in the concordance of the Bible. Amen is used many times through out the whole Bible.

As you work your way through making a prayer shawl you are busy praying for the person who will receive it and their situation. After you complete the shawl and praying, think of laying your hand on the shawl and saying, "Amen" So be it, Lord Jesus, so be it.

# PONDERINGS

"

"

# PONDERINGS

"

"

# MINISTRY

> " This garment was made for you with love.
> The stitches were woven with prayers for you
> to bless you,
> heal you,
> and comfort you.
> May you rest quietly in it's soft warmth
> as you feel the
> nearness of the God who made you
> and promised to never leave you. "

This is the verse we attach to each of the prayer shawls that we give. There are many variations of this verse but they are all intended to minister to the person receiving the shawl. We pray as we make the shawl that the person receiving the shawl may feel the touch of Jesus' arms around them when they use the shawl as well as the many prayers of many people going before the throne of God in intercession for that person.

Elderly people who have lived alone for many years, widows and widowers all talk about how they miss the touch of a human being. We underestimate the power of a hug or touch to lonely people.

After Jesus had been in the wilderness for 40 days and endured the temptation of Satan, He was ministered to by angels. Matthew 4:11 tells us, *"Then the devil left Him, and the angels came and attended Him."* The Son of God needed the angels to minister to Him. He needed food, water, rest and peace. After being pestered by Satan for 40 days, He must have been emotionally as well as physically exhausted.

There are many different forms of ministry that we give to each other and what our needs are. We usually sit in the same bench in church and have the same people sitting around us. We have a "Mentos Ministry" in our bench. We bring Mentos and share with the people in our bench. That may be a stretch on the word ministry but it gets us to interact with the people around us and we reach out to each other in different aspects of each other's lives. It has developed into an accountability to each other if we are absent from church.

May we each be aware of the different calling on our gifts that we can minister to one another in the name of Jesus.

# PONDERINGS

"

"

# PONDERINGS

"

"

# PERFECTION

*❝ Be perfect, therefore, as your heavenly Father is perfect. ❞* —Matthew 5:48

Joni Erickson Tada is a well known gospel singer and speaker. She had a diving accident as a teenager and has been paralyzed from the neck down since then. Recently I heard her speak about heaven and she said people assumed she would anticipate a perfect body and be able to walk and dance. But she was anticipating heaven and having a perfect heart.

We anticipate heaven for human, earthly desires. Having a slender body, not have to wear glasses or not having aches and pains. But have you thought about having a perfect heart with pure attitudes? Colossians 3:23-24 tell us, *"Whatever you do, work at it with all your heart, as working for the Lord, not for men, since you know that you will receive an inheritance from the Lord as a reward. It is the Lord Christ you are serving."*

We long for perfection in our lives and it is so easy to not do something because we don't feel we do it well enough. Making a prayer shawl doesn't require perfect workmanship as much as it requires a willing heart. We focus on the tangible part of the shawl—if our stitches are even, the edges are even, if the colors are right and if it blocks out square. God is looking for faithful workers not perfect ones.

God focuses on the heart and spirit that the shawl is being made with. We don't always achieve a perfect heart but God honor's our efforts to be like Him. Don't let perfection steal your joy in making a prayer shawl for one of God's hurting people.

# PONDERINGS

"

"

# PONDERINGS

"

"

# DIVERSITY

**" You are the light of the world. "** —Matthew 5:14

Recently a friend was very surprised to find out that prayer shawls could be crocheted as well as knitted and didn't need to be made from a certain brand of yarn. God blesses hookers too! We have made shawls out of fleece as well. Praying can be done while tying knots in fleece as well as knitting or crocheting yarn. One of the local churches has a group of ladies that piece together a lap robe top from fabric and then have different people tie it with yarn and pray while they are doing it. It is the prayerful attitude in which the shawl, lap robe or blanket is made that is the key to purpose of the item.

Jesus was very inclusive in His ministry here on earth. He reached out to rich and poor, slave or free man, men and women, old and young alike. They didn't all receive Him or welcome Him but He reached out to them all equally.

It is so easy for us to get caught up in our holy huddles of people who believe like we do, behave like we do, think like we do and not reach out to others. In Genesis 11 the people after the flood decided to build a tower and live closely together and not be scattered over the face of the earth. God confused their language so they couldn't understand each other and scattered them over all the earth.

God certainly wants us to have friends and close relationships but it certainly broadens our world to have friends from different backgrounds, religions, etc. We need to be willing to step out of our comfort zone. A word of caution would be to surround ourselves with strong Christian relationships that help us to hold ourselves accountable to our Lord. Look at what diversity Jesus' disciples were from. Tax collectors and fishermen were some of their occupations that we know of. Jesus was the son of a carpenter.

We are to be salt and light in this world. Our making of shawls, in whatever fabric or yarn, and whether knitted or crocheted is our way of reaching out to others.

# PONDERINGS

"

"

# PONDERINGS

"

"

# MULTITASKING

Throughout His ministry, Jesus was busy multitasking. He would be walking along and teaching and then someone would reach out to be healed or ask a question. In Luke 8:43-44 a woman who had suffered with a bleeding problem for 12 years reached out just to touch the hem of Jesus' garment and was healed. Jesus was aware who had touched Him and that she was healed.

We knitters and crocheters do a lot of multitasking. We knit and crochet while we watch TV, ride in the car, ride the exercise bike and many more activities. Watching TV can put you to sleep if you don't keep your hands busy! While we are watching TV and keeping our hands busy we are thinking of the next project we want to work on. Most importantly we are praying for whoever will receive the shawl we are working on.

When Jesus was on the cross He was aware of the two people on the crosses beside Him. When we are in pain, our world shrinks around us and we are mostly just aware of ourselves and our pain and discomfort. Jesus was not only enduring human suffering and death but the separation from God. Yet Jesus reached out from His incredible pain to those around Him. He forgave those who were crucifying Him, addressed His mother's care and told the thief, *"I tell you the truth, today you will be with Me in paradise"* (Luke 23:43). He did request a drink and had His physical need for thirst met. He was multitasking even in His final hours.

In all the business of life, may our multitasking focus on reaching out to others. We need to evaluate what we are multitasking about and work on simplifying our lives by cutting out some of the business. Our focus needs to be on reaching lost and hurting people for Jesus.

# PONDERINGS

"

"

# PONDERINGS

"

"

# BAG LADIES

Have you ever noticed how many "things" we have to take along with us in different bags? We have a bag for swimming things, a bag for Bible study, a bag that we take to work that contains snacks for the day, reading material and who knows what else. And that is in addition to the purse we carry that has everything but the kitchen sink in it. For that matter, as heavy as that purse is, maybe the kitchen sink IS in there! We even pay extra to fly on commercial airlines to get our bags with our possessions along

We knitters and crocheters certainly like our bags as well. We have different bags with different projects in them. We like to have those busy bags along with us in case we get a few minutes to add a few stitches to our project.

When reading in the gospels about Jesus' life and ministry there is never a reference to getting Jesus' luggage or baggage along. He traveled light and was dependent on others for a place to sleep at night . Matthew 8:20 tells us *"Jesus replied, 'Foxes have holes and birds of the air have nests, but the Son of Man has no place to lay His head."* He was born in someone else's barn and was buried in a borrowed tomb.

We are in bondage to the things of this world. We have physical baggage as well as emotional baggage that we are dealing with. We bring our baggage to Jesus in our prayers and when we are finished praying, we pick them back up again. We need to read the words of Matthew 11:28-30 again, *"Come to Me, all you who are weary and burdened, and I will give you rest. Take My yoke upon you and learn from Me, for I am gentle and humble in heart, and you will find rest for your souls. For My yoke is easy and My burden is light."*

# PONDERINGS

"

"

149

# PONDERINGS

"

"

# LITTLE IS MUCH

**❝** He also saw a poor widow put in two very small copper coins. **❞** Luke 21:2

It has recently been expressed to me that people feel inadequate to be part of the prayer shawl ministry because it takes them so long to make one shawl. They don't feel like they are contributing very much. Every single shawl is of great value!

The text from Luke goes on to say, *"this poor widow has put in more than all the others. All these people gave their gifts out of their wealth; but she out of her poverty put in all she had to live on."* We can look at the financial gift that one shawl is but we also need to see the gift of time, willingness and the blessing the person making the shawl receives as well as the person receiving the shawl.

We will never know what small things do in God's kingdom. The way we live our lives, our attitude, and words of encouragement to someone along the way can all be part of bringing that person to accept Jesus into their heart. The one shawl that took you nearly a year to make may be just the right blessing for someone.  Little is much when God is in it!

Jesus saw the monetary price this woman was willing to pay but He also saw her heart.  He saw her willing spirit as well as what sacrifice of pride it may have cost her to give such a small amount in front of other people. II Corinthians 8:12 tells us, *"For if the willingness is there, the gift is acceptable according to what one has, not according to what he does not have."* What matters is the willingness, which is the motive of true generosity, no matter how small the amount that can be given.

# PONDERINGS

"

"

# PONDERINGS

"

"

# DIFFERENT PATTERNS

When starting a new project, it is so easy to slip into an old tested and tried pattern. We need to challenge ourselves by trying out new patterns from time to time. Our comfort zone is challenged.

Matthew 4:18-22 tells us about Jesus calling some of the disciples. Twice it tells us about two brothers who *"immediately left the boat and their father and followed Him."* They didn't hardly even think about what they were leaving or what they were getting themselves into. They just dropped everything and followed Jesus. That would majorly challenge a comfort zone! The call to discipleship is definite and demands a response of total commitment. Simon and Andrew had encountered Jesus previously with John the Baptist (John 2:40-42) when Jesus renames Simon to Peter. So they were aware of Jesus and His ministry before actually being called and following Jesus.

Bringing a shawl to someone we don't know is also a challenge. We go, expecting to bless someone and frequently we are blessed by the encounter. First we need to be willing to be God's hands to make and deliver the shawl.

Psalm 41:1 tells us, *"Blessed is he who has regard for the weak."*

We need to be willing to stretch and grow by using new patterns and make ourselves available for what God wants from us.

# PONDERINGS

"

"

CPSIA information can be obtained at www.ICGtesting.com
Printed in the USA
BVOW03s2250131214

379144BV00009B/334/P